GYMNASTIC EVENTS

by Jason Page

CONTENTS

Crabtree Publishing Company
www.crabtreebooks.com

Editor: Robert Walker
Proofreader: Mike Hodge
Acknowledgements: We would like to thank Ian Hodge, Rosalind Beckman and Elizabeth Wiggans for their assistance.
Cartoons by: John Alston
Picture Credits: t = top, b = bottom, l = left, r = right, OFC = outside front cover, OBC = outside back cover, IFC = front cover
Action-plus: 20/21 (main pic), 29tr, 28/29 (main pic).
Allsport: 2/3c, 5b, 6/7 (main), 11b, 16/17

(main pic), 22/23c, 24/25b, 26/27 (main pic), 31tr. Clive Brunskill/ Getty Images: 13. Adrian Dennis/ AFP/ Getty Images: 20tl. Stephane De Sakutin/ AFP/ Getty Images: 17c. Empics: IFC, 2b, 4/5c, 6c, 8/9 (main pic), 10/11 (main pic), 12 (main pic), 14/15 (main pic), 18/19 (main pic), 27c, 30/31 (main pic). Doug Pensinger/ Getty Images: 15t. Rick Rycroft/ AP/ PA Photos: 18. Sporting Pictures UK: 8t, 22l. Neil Tingle/ Action Plus: OFC.
Picture research by Image Select

Library and Archives Canada Cataloguing in Publication

Page, Jason
    Gymnastic events / Jason Page.

(The Olympic sports)
Includes index.
ISBN 978-0-7787-4015-5 (bound).--ISBN 978-0-7787-4032-2 (pbk.)

    1. Gymnastics--Juvenile literature. 2. Olympics--Juvenile literature.
I. Title. II. Series: Page, Jason. Olympic sports

GV461.3.P33 2008   j796.44   C2008-900973-8

Library of Congress Cataloging-in-Publication Data

Page, Jason.
  Gymnastics events / Jason Page.
    p. cm. -- (The Olympic sports)
  Includes index.
  ISBN-13: 978-0-7787-4015-5 (rlb)
  ISBN-10: 0-7787-4015-3 (rlb)
  ISBN-13: 978-0-7787-4032-2 (pb)
  ISBN-10: 0-7787-4032-3 (pb)
  1. Gymnastics--Juvenile literature. 2. Olympics--Juvenile literature.
I. Title. II. Series.

GV461.3.P345 2008
796.44--dc22

2008004909

Crabtree Publishing Company

www.crabtreebooks.com   1-800-387-7650

Published in Canada
Crabtree Publishing
616 Welland Ave.
St. Catharines, Ontario
L2M 5V6

Published in the United States
Crabtree Publishing
PMB16A
350 Fifth Ave., Suite 3308
New York, NY 10118

GYMNASTIC EVENTS

Gymnastics is one of only five sports that have been included in every single modern Olympics — the others are athletics, swimming, fencing, and cycling.

In 1976, 18,000 spectators watched the final of the women's individual combined events — the biggest crowd ever at an Olympic gymnastics event. If all these people stood on each other's shoulders, they would be 3.5 times as tall as Mount Everest!

NAKED TRUTH

Soldiers in ancient Greece were taught gymnastics as part of their military training. In fact, the word "gymnastics" comes from the Greek word *gymnos* which means naked, because in ancient times all gymnasts performed in the nude!

Dancers depicting ancient Greek athletes, Atlanta, 1996

Nadia Comaneci (ROM)

There are three different kinds of gymnastic events at the Olympic Games. They are known as the three "disciplines" of gymnastics and are called: artistic gymnastics, rhythmic gymnastics, and trampoline. The trampoline is a relatively new event that appeared for the first time at the Olympic Games in 2000.

OLYMPICS FACT FILE

The Olympic Games were first held in Olympia, in ancient Greece, around 3,000 years ago. They took place every four years until they were abolished in 393 A.D.

A Frenchman named Pierre de Coubertin (1863–1937) revived the Games, and the first modern Olympics were held in Athens in 1896.

The modern Games have been held every four years since 1896, except in 1916, 1940, and 1944, due to war. Special 10th-anniversary Games took place in 1906.

The symbol of the Olympic Games is five interlocking colored rings. Together, they represent the five original continents from which athletes came to compete in the Games.

SEVEN OF THE BEST

At the Games in 1976, 14-year-old Nadia Comaneci (ROM) became the first person in Olympic history ever to score a "perfect 10," the highest score possible in a gymnastic event. But she didn't just do it once — she went on to achieve seven perfect performances.

MODERN GYMNASTICS

The first modern gymnastic equipment was designed and built by a German school teacher named Friedrich Jahn in the early 1800s. The sport soon caught on in schools and athletic clubs, and its popularity ensured that it was included in the first modern Olympic Games. Women competed in gymnastic events at the Olympics for the first time in 1928.

ARTISTIC EVENTS

Athletes climb, jump, and swing on different apparatus in the artistic events.

Alexei Nemov (RUS)

THREE IN ONE

The artistic competition is divided into three parts — team events, individual combined events, and single apparatus events. In the team and combined competitions, the gymnasts perform on all the apparatus; in the single apparatus events, just one piece of equipment is used.

ON APPARATUS

Eight different kinds of apparatus are used in the 14 different artistic events. Men compete on six apparatus (pommel horse, still rings, vault, parallel bars, horizontal bar, and floor exercise); the women on four (vault, uneven bars, balance beam, and floor exercise).

SUPER STATS

Between 1956 and 1964, Larisa Latynina (URS) won 18 Olympic medals (including nine golds), making her the most successful competitor in Olympic history.

Alexei Nemov, a member of Russia's winning men's team at the 1996 Games, performing on the still rings.

SCORING

All artistic gymnastic events are scored by two panels of judges. One panel is made up of two judges, who give each performance a score based on the difficulty of the routine. The harder the skills performed by the gymnast, the higher the score. The second panel, with six judges, assesses how well the moves were performed. This panel starts with a score of 10 and deducts points for any errors that the gymnast made. The final score is calculated by adding the two scores.

Tatiana Gutsu (EUN)

DID YOU KNOW?

The youngest-ever medallist in a gymnastic event was 10-year-old Dimitrios Loundras (GRE), who won a bronze medal on the parallel bars at the Games in 1896.

Since 1984, all male gymnasts must be 16 years old and female gymnasts must be at least 15 years old to compete in the Games.

The oldest person ever to win a medal in the gymnastics competition was 46-year-old Ethel Seymour (GBR), who won a bronze in 1928 in the women's team event.

A fraction of a point can make all the difference. In 1992, Tatiana Gutsu (EUN) beat Shannon Miller (USA) by just 0.012 points — the smallest-ever margin of victory in an Olympic gymnastic event!

Each apparatus demands a different combination of strength, balance, and agility. To become an all-around champion like Li Xiaoshuang (CHN), gymnasts must master them all.

¿? Each country may enter one team. A team is made up of six gymnasts.

¿? The USSR won the women's team event eight times in a row from 1952–1980.

WHAT A HERO

If there was an Olympic medal for bravery, it would have been won by Shun Fujimoto (JPN) at the 1976 Games. Fujimoto broke his kneecap while competing in the men's team event. However, he knew that if he withdrew from the competition he would ruin his team's chances of winning a medal, so he kept his painful injury secret and went on to compete in two more events. Thanks to Fujimoto, Japan won the gold!

INDIVIDUAL CHAMPIONS

Here the gymnasts are competing on their own, rather than as a member of a team. The winner is known as the "all-round" champion and is regarded as the best gymnast at the Games.

US women's team, Atlanta 1996

TAKE A BOW

The US women's team celebrate after winning the gold medal in front of their home crowd at the 1996 Games in Atlanta. It was the USA's first-ever victory in the women's team event.

TEAM & COMBINED EVENTS

Li Xiaoshuang (CHN)

In the team and individual combined events, competitors must perform on all the different apparatus.

EVERYTHING'S OPTIONAL!

Previously at the Olympics, the gymnasts had to perform twice on each apparatus. Once to do a compulsory routine that was set by the judges, the second time to do an optional routine which they had composed themselves. But in recent years, the Olympic compulsory routines have been dropped and Olympic gymnasts now only compete in "optionals."

TEAM TOTALS

A team is made up of six gymnasts. In the team qualifying competition, five athletes compete on each event and four scores count. In the team finals, three athletes compete on each event and every score counts towards the team total. Only the scores from the team final competition are considered when deciding the team medals.

SUPER STATS

The former Soviet Union dominated the gymnastic events at the Games. Even though the USSR ceased to exist in 1991, it remains top of the medals table to this day. Its medal tally of 204 is still twice the number of its closest rivals Japan and the USA.

Women's team: ROMANIA / **Women's individual combined:** Carly Patterson, USA

SINGLE APPARATUS: FLOOR

The floor is the only single apparatus event in which men and women compete on the same apparatus in exactly the same way.

ANIMAL OLYMPIANS

When it comes to performing magnificent jumps and twists, even an Olympic gymnast can't match a killer whale. These mighty mammals love showing off their acrobatic skills and can leap 19.7 feet (6 m) out of the water.

SOME SOMERSAULT!

Vladimir Gogoladze (URS) turned Olympic gymnastics upside down during the floor exercises at the 1988 Games. To the amazement of the crowd and judges, he performed a spectacular triple somersault — the first in the history of the Games!

Vladimir Gogoladze (URS)

STAR QUALITY

The floor exercises test the four essential qualities that all great gymnasts need: flexibility, grace, strength, and balance. The 2004 Olympic women's floor champion, Catalina Ponor (ROM), announced her retirement in 2007.

MAT FACTS

The floor exercises are performed on a large mat made from a springy material suitable for both powerful take-offs and soft landings. Around the edge of the mat is a 3.3 feet-wide (1 m) "safety border." Gymnasts must not step on the border except when approaching or leaving the mat.

ON THE FLOOR

In the floor exercises, gymnasts must perform a continuous series of acrobatic movements. These include somersaults, handstands, turns, leaps, and dance elements. In the women's event, each routine must last between 60 and 90 seconds. The men's routines must be between 50 and 70 seconds long.

DID YOU KNOW?

- The women's floor exercises are performed to music but the men's routines are not.
- In 1992, the women's floor exercises were won by Lavinia Milosovici (ROM) with a "perfect 10" performance.
- Competitors are penalized if they finish their routine outside the time limits.

Lilia Podkopayeva (UKR)

Women's event: Catalina Ponor (ROM)

SINGLE APPARATUS: POMMEL HORSE

The pommel horse is a rectangular block on four legs which looks a bit like a headless horse — hence its name!

SADDLE UP!

The top of the horse is just over three feet (1 m) high and nearly 5 feet (1.5 m) long, with two raised handles in the center known as "pommels." Only men compete in this event.

Chalking hands to improve grip

SUPER STATS

How does the size of a pommel horse compare with the height of the back of a real horse?

Pommel horse — 41.3 inches (105 cm) high
The average horse — 59 inches (150 cm) high
The tallest horse — 69 inches (175 cm) high
The shortest breed of horse — 30 inches (76 cm) high

SCISSOR LEGS

On the pommel horse, the gymnast must support his weight using his hands while he performs a series of continuous swinging movements with his legs. One move is known as the "scissors." Here the gymnast has one leg on either side of the horse. As he swings from side to side, he lets go with one hand and switches his legs. The leg at the front of the horse moves to the back and the leg at the back of the horse moves to the front.

A DUSTING DOWN

Before performing on the horse, competitors dip their hands into a bowl of magnesium carbonate. This is a fine white powder which absorbs sweat and helps gymnasts to grip the pommels without their hands sticking or slipping.

DID YOU KNOW?

The pommel horse is sometimes also called the "side horse."

Gymnasts are expected to use the whole length of the horse and to travel up and down it on their hands!

In the apparatus finals, the top eight gymnasts on each event compete for medals. Only two gymnasts from each country may advance to each apparatus final.

SHARING THE GLORY

There has been a triple tie for a gold medal on only two occasions at the Olympics and both were in the pommel horse event! In 1948, three Finnish gymnasts shared the gold. Forty years later, in 1988, Dimitry Bilozertchev (URS) shared the gold with gymnasts from Bulgaria and Hungary.

Dimitry Bilozertchev (URS)

SILVER: Marius Urzica (ROM) / **BRONZE**: Takehiro Kashima (JPN)

Just before each performance, gymnasts coat the soles of their feet or slippers in magnesium carbonate to prevent them from slipping.

Gymnasts on the bar are allowed to compete barefoot but some prefer to wear slippers.

Bandages are strapped around injured muscles and joints to provide support.

Dominique Moceanu (USA)

BALANCING ACT

Gymnasts must perform a routine lasting between 50 and 70 seconds on the narrow balance beam, without falling off! Competitors are expected to use the whole length of the beam and typical moves include jumps, leaps, turns, handsprings, and somersaults. Only women compete in this event at the Games.

DID YOU KNOW?

If a gymnast falls off the beam, she will automatically have 0.8 points deducted from her score.

Gymnasts also have points deducted from their score if they behave in an unsportsmanlike manner.

Coaches are forbidden to talk to their gymnasts while they are performing.

Gymnasts wear stretchy leotards that allow them to move freely.

The beam is a horizontal wooden bar nearly four feet (1.2 m) above the ground. It is 33 feet (10 m) long and just four inches (10 cm) wide.

Dominique Moceanu won a gold medal at the 1996 Games in the women's team event.

2004 OLYMPIC MEDALISTS: GOLD: Catalina Ponor (ROM)

SINGLE APPARATUS: BALANCE BEAM

Walking along the narrow balance beam looks hard enough – just imagine doing cartwheels and somersaults as well!

IT TAKES STYLE

On the beam, as with the other all-female events, balance and agility count for more than sheer strength. Artistry and a sense of style are also very important. This is because, in addition to looking at how well each individual move is executed, the judges also take into consideration the artistic effect of the performance as a whole.

ANIMAL OLYMPIANS

If there was a gold medal for balancing in the Animal Olympics, it would be won by a spider. Spiders can walk along a single strand of the silk which they use to build their webs – even though it's less than 0.04 inches (1 mm) wide!

Catalina Ponor (ROM)

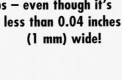
The 2004 Olympic balance beam champion is Catalina Ponor (ROM).

SILVER: Carly Patterson (USA) / **BRONZE:** Alexandra Eremia (ROM)

SINGLE APPARATUS: HORIZONTAL BAR

Competitors in the horizontal bar event really get things swinging at the Games!

WHAT A PERFORMANCE!

Competitors in this event grip the bar using either one or two hands but some of the most spectacular skills involve letting go completely, performing a twist or somersault in the air then grabbing hold of the bar again. Only men compete in this event.

ANIMAL OLYMPIANS

Gibbons are the greatest swingers in the animal kingdom. Using their long, powerful arms they cover almost 10 feet (3 m) in a single swing!

Gymnasts' pants have foot straps to prevent the bottoms of the pants being pulled up.

Male gymnasts usually wear lightweight slippers, although they may compete barefoot if they prefer.

Male gymnasts wear a fitted, sleeveless shirt.

Leather straps called hand-grips support the wrist and help the gymnast to grip the bar.

POLE TO POLE

The horizontal bar is a 8.2 foot-long (2.5 m) pole mounted on two tall stands 8.2 feet (2.5 m) high. Although it's made from highly polished steel, it's actually quite flexible.

Igor Cassina (ITA) is the 2004 Olympic gold medalist in the horizontal bar event.

Male gymnasts wear fitted pants made from a stretchy material.

GOLDEN BOY

Vitaly Scherbo (EUN/BLR) won six gold medals at the 1992 Games. In doing so, he set the record for the most gold medals ever won by a gymnast at one Games! At the 1996 Olympics he added four bronzes to his medal collection.

DID YOU KNOW?

Vitaly Scherbo represented the Commonwealth of Independent States (EUN) at the 1992 Games; as this no longer existed by the time of the 1996 Games, he represented his native Belarus instead.

Nobody knows the name of the gymnast who won the bronze medal on the horizontal bar at the 1896 Games.

The men's gymnastic events used to include a rope climbing race. This was held for the last time in 1932.

BRONZE: Isao Yoneda (JPN)

DID YOU KNOW?

♫ The uneven bars are also known as the asymmetrical bars.

♫ Competitors on the horizontal and uneven bars must keep moving all the time — they are not allowed to come to a stop.

♫ At just over 8 feet (2.45 m) high, the tallest of the two bars is about twice as tall as an average 7-year-old child.

HAPPY LANDINGS

In all the artistic events (apart from the floor events), the gymnasts must "dismount'"(get off the apparatus) at the end of their routines. Competitors try to make their dismounts as spectacular as possible by launching themselves into the air and performing somersaults and twists before landing. All dismounts must end with the gymnast in the finish position, shown right.

Li Lu (CHN)

Hands and fingers in a graceful pose

Arms outstretched

Chest thrust outward

Feet together

SINGLE APPARATUS: UNEVEN BARS

While men perform on a single horizontal bar, women gymnasts have not one but two bars to contend with!

THE SECOND PARALLEL

The uneven parallel bars is an event for women gymnasts only. The apparatus consists of two horizontal bars set at different heights with a space between them. The taller bar is just over 8 feet (2.45 m) above the ground while the lower bar is 5.4 feet (1.65 m) high. An average nine-year-old child, standing on tiptoe, would just be able to reach it.

SUPER STATS

Russia and the former Soviet Union are at the top of the league in the uneven bars event with three golds. Next are China, East Germany, and Hungary who have each won two golds.

SILVER: Terin Humphrey (USA) / **BRONZE:** Courtney Kupets (USA)

SINGLE APPARATUS: STILL RINGS

The rings event is the supreme test of strength. But muscle power alone isn't enough — control and grace are needed, too!

ANIMAL OLYMPIANS

Routines on the rings last less than five minutes, but bats hang upside down for most of the day. They even sleep in this position!

RINGING ROUND

This event is for men only and is performed on two rings suspended from cables about 8 feet (2.5 m) above the floor. Gymnasts must keep the rings as still as possible while performing their routine. It requires tremendous physical strength — just take a look at the bulging muscles of Dimosthenis Tampakos (GRE)!

2004 OLYMPIC MEDALISTS: GOLD: Dimosthenis Tampakos (GRE)

Yik Siang Loke (MAS)

NEED A LIFT?

On the rings and the horizontal bar, a coach or teammate may lift the competitor up so that he can reach the apparatus. This is the only occasion where a gymnast is allowed to receive help without being penalized.

HOLD STILL

Routines on the rings usually include a number of holding moves in which the competitor remains perfectly still for at least two seconds. One of the most difficult holding moves is known as the cross — gymnasts move their bodies in an upright position with their arms out sideways. In this picture, Yik Siang Loke (MAS) shows how it's done!

SAFETY FIRST

In addition to the safety mats which are placed underneath the rings, people known as "spotters" are positioned nearby. Their job is to try to catch the gymnast if he falls. However, a competitor who receives help from a spotter automatically has 0.8 points deducted from his score.

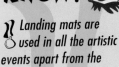

DID YOU KNOW?

Landing mats are used in all the artistic events apart from the floor.

At the Games in 1952, gymnasts from the Soviet Union won gold, silver, and bronze medals on the rings.

In 1912 and 1920, the Games included a team event for men known as the "Swedish system." In this event, men performed routines with hoops, clubs, and balls.

SINGLE APPARATUS: VAULT

The vault is an event for both men and women. Vaulting requires power, strength, and control.

TABLE TALK

Both men and women compete in the vault, using the same equipment. Gymnasts vault over a piece of equipment called the vault table. For men the vault table is set at a height of 4.4 feet (1.35 m), while for women it is set at a height of 4.1 feet (1.25 m).

Gervasio Deferr (ESP)

2004 OLYMPIC CHAMPIONS: Men's event: Gervasio Deferr (ESP)

JUMP FOR IT

NEED TO SEE PICTURE TO WRITE TEXT

To generate the speed and power needed to perform a vault, gymnasts run up a runway. The runway is usually 82 feet (25 m) long.

A SECOND GO

Vault routines are quick but complicated. Gymnasts gather speed running toward the vaulting table, and then launch themselves off the springboard toward the vault. Gymnasts use their hands to push off the vault and propel themselves into the air. They then perform a combination of twists and somersaults before landing on the mat. Gymnasts are judged on their body position, the height they achieve during the vault, and the distance of the landing from the vault table.

ANIMAL OLYMPIANS

When it comes to vaulting at the Animal Olympics, frogs would leap at the chance to win a gold medal. African sharp-nosed frogs can vault across more than 16 feet (5 m) — that's longer than a family car.

Women's event: Monica Rosu (ROM)

SINGLE APPARATUS: PARALLEL BARS

The parallel bars event demands the strength of the rings and the agility of the horizontal bar.

Nikolai Andrianov (URS)

GOLDEN GREAT

Nikolai Andrianov (URS) holds the record for the most medals ever won by a male competitor in any sport at the Olympic Games. Between 1972 and 1980, he won 15 medals in gymnastic events, including a silver on the parallel bars in 1976. He also shares the record for being the most successful male gymnast, having won seven gold medals.

SUPER STATS

Japan and the USSR head the medals table in this event, both having won it four times. Switzerland has three victories, while the USA and Germany have each won two gold medals.

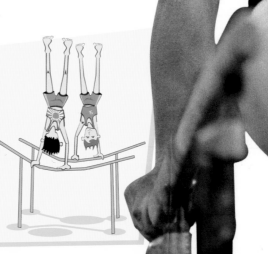

2004 OLYMPIC MEDALISTS: GOLD: Valeri Goncharov (UKR)

AGILITY & STRENGTH

The gymnasts demonstrate their agility and balance by performing twists, handstands and swinging moves on the bars. They also perform holding moves and other moves which are done very slowly. These are designed to show off their strength and control.

RAIL WAY

The two wooden rails used in this event are both 5.7 feet (1.75 m) high and about 1.6 feet (0.5 m) apart. Competitors must support their weight using only their arms. This requires incredible muscle power, and is a men-only event.

During a holding move the gymnast must remain completely still. Vitaly Scherbo (EUN), who won the gold in 1992, makes it look easy here, but this move takes great strength and concentration.

DID YOU KNOW?

A US gymnast called George Eyser won six medals at the Games in 1904, including a gold on the parallel bars, despite the fact that he had a wooden leg.

The first-ever gymnastics gold medal was awarded to the German team, who won the parallel bars event in 1896.

In 1972, all the medals for the parallel bars were won by Japanese gymnasts.

SILVER: Hiroyuki Tomita (JPN) / **BRONZE:** Li Xiaopeng (CHN)

The two clubs are bottle-shaped with a thick end and a thin end. They must be the same length and weight.

The rope must be made from hemp or a similar material. The length of the rope used depends on the height of the gymnast.

The ball measures close t̶ inches (19–20 cm) It can be made o̶̶ rubber or soft pla̶ must weigh at le̶ pounds (400

The hoop must weigh at least 0.7 pounds (300 g) and measure 31–35 inches (80–90 cm) across. It can be made of either wood or plastic.

The ribbon is made from a strip of material nearly 23 feet (7 m) long, attached to a short stick, around 22 inches (50–60 cm) long, which the competitor holds.

IN CONTACT

The gymnast's performance must end precisely on the last note of the music. At the end of her routine, the gymnast must be touching the apparatus, although she can use any part of the body she likes.

Alina Stoica (ROM)

RHYTHMIC: INDIVIDUAL

Unlike artistic gymnastics, all the events in rhythmic gymnastics are for women only.

ROUTINE WORK

In rhythmic gymnastics, the routines are always accompanied by music and many of the steps and movements performed by the competitors actually come from ballet. The gymnasts must keep the apparatus moving all the time and each routine must last between 75 and 90 seconds. A penalty of 0.05 points is deducted for every second a gymnast performs over or under this time limit.

LEARN THE LINGO

These ballet terms are also used in rhythmic gymnastics:

Plié – bending knees outward, with the back held straight

Jeté – jumping from one leg to another

Arabesque – standing on one leg with the other leg held out at a right angle

Attitude – standing on one leg with the other leg held out backwards with the knee bent

SPOT THE DIFFERENCE

The difference between artistic and rhythmic gymnastics is simple — rhythmic gymnastics are performed with an apparatus, rather than on one. In the individual event each gymnast performs four times, each time with a different piece of apparatus. There are five altogether: a ball, rope, ribbon, pair of clubs, and a hoop.

SILVER: Irina Tchachina (RUS) / **BRONZE:** Anna Bessonova (UKR)

RHYTHMIC: TEAM

Diana Popova (BUL)

A team event in the rhythmic gymnastics competition was introduced at the 1996 Olympics.

TEAM WORK

Each team is made up of five gymnasts who perform on the mat together. Every team does two different routines. In the first routine, all the gymnasts perform using clubs; in the second, two team members use hoops while the other three use ribbons.

WINNING RIBBONS

Competitors performing with the ribbon must keep the material in constant, fluid motion throughout the performance. One of the most impressive and daring moves involves throwing the ribbon up high into the air then dancing across the mat and catching it as it falls to the ground.

SUPER STATS

The ribbon used by gymnasts in rhythmic events is about three times as long as an elephant's trunk!

Rhythmic gymnasts are scored by three panels of judges. Here's how the scoring works:

1) The "technical" panel award up to four points (five in the individual event) according to the difficulty of the routine.

2) The "artistic" panel award up to six points (up to five in the individual event) for the beauty and originality of the performance.

3) The "execution" panel award up to 10 points according to how well each move is performed — the more mistakes they spot, the lower the gymnasts' score.

DID YOU KNOW?

♫ Rhythmic gymnastics are performed on a large mat surrounded by a "safety area."

♫ In the team event, each score is out of 20; in the individual event, the points awarded by the judges are halved to give a score out of 10.

♫ At the 1996 Games the Spanish beat the Bulgarian team into second place by just 0.067 points!

Yelena Vitrichenko (UKR)

BEND & STRETCH

Rhythmic gymnasts bend over backwards to please the judges — literally! In most routines, you'll see incredible stretches and other moves designed to show off the flexibility and suppleness of the gymnast's body.

DID YOU KNOW?

The bed on a trampoline is very thin — just 0.2 inches (6 mm) thick!

Every routine performed in the trampoline events must contain 10 recognized moves.

The first purpose-built modern trampoline was built in the 1930s.

A padded safety platform helps to protect competitors who accidentally bounce off.

Markings on the trampoline help the competitor to land on the centre of the bed.

The springy part of the trampoline is called the "bed." It's made of a material, usually nylon, which is both strong and stretchy.

Trampoline

THE BOUNCIEST NATIONS

Trampolining is a relatively new Olympic sport and has only featured in two Games: Sydney and Athens. So far, Russia has been the best nation, winning two gold medals and one silver.

ROUND & ROUND

The trampolining events consist of two rounds. The first is a qualifying round in which each competitor must perform two routines. The first routine is compulsory (the moves are set by the judges and must be performed in order); the second routine is optional (competitors decide which moves they will perform and in which order). The second round decides the medals and consists of one optional routine only.

The bed is stretched across a strong metal frame 5.05 meters long and 2.91 meters wide.

TRAMPOLINE

At the Beijing Olympics there will be two events, one for men and one for women.

BOUNCING THROUGH HISTORY

The trampoline is named after a French circus performer, called Du Trampoline, who lived about 200 years ago. Apparently, he came up with the idea of using the safety net from the circus high wire act to bounce up and down while performing acrobatics.

Ian Ross (GBR)

Competitors wear the same clothes as other gymnasts, together with socks or gymnastic slippers.

The bed of the trampoline is raised 3.8 feet (1.15 m) off the ground.

SUPER STATS

Trampolinists can bounce up to 20 feet (6 m) in the air — that's like jumping over a giraffe!

TRAMPOLINE (CONTINUED)

With the success of individual trampoline events, maybe a team event will also one day feature on the Olympic programme.

WHAT'S THE SCORE?

Like other gymnastic events, trampolinists are awarded marks according to the difficulty of the moves they attempt and how well they perform them. Seven judges score each routine: two judges award points for difficulty while the other five score the execution of each move. The maximum score for a faultless performance is usually around 45 points.

ANIMAL OLYMPIANS

When it comes to bouncing, nothing can beat the klipspringer. This amazing African antelope can jump more than seven meters into the air – which beats even an Olympic trampolinist!

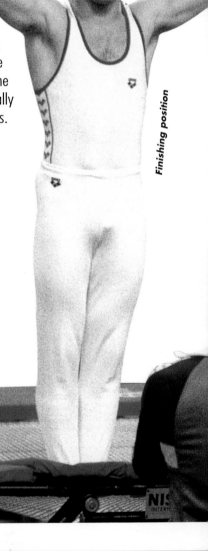

Finishing position

MAKE YOUR MOVE

Top trampolinists perform a dazzling display of moves, including forward and backward somersaults and twists. They also combine moves, for example a quadruple somersault with a twist is known as a "quadriffis."

BOING BOING!

Competitors are allowed to bounce by landing on the front and backs of their bodies, provided they don't touch the trampoline with their hands. However, when bouncing upright, they must land on both feet at the same time. Failing to do so will result in an automatic penalty and 0.3 points will be deducted from their score.

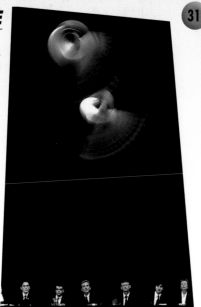

Somersaults

NO WOBBLING

At the end of a routine, gymnasts must stand on the trampoline with their feet together and arms outstretched, as this picture shows. They must maintain this position for at least 3 seconds — points are deducted if they wobble!

DID YOU KNOW?

♫ Trampolinists remain in the air for up to two whole seconds between bounces!

♫ Trampolines were used in the 1970s to help train astronauts for space missions in order to get them used to being upside down!

♫ The rules state that trampoline competitions must be held in a room with a ceiling that's at least 26 feet (8 m) high!

SILVER: Karen Cockburn (CAN) / **BRONZE:** Shanshan Huang (CHN)

INDEX

COUNTRY ABBREVIATIONS

BLR - Belarus
CHN - China
EUN - Unified team
(Commonwealth of Independent
States, 1992)
GBR - Great Britain
GER - Germany
GRE - Greece
ITA - Italy
JPN - Japan
MAS - Malaysia
ROM - Romania
RUS - Russia
SUI - Switzerland

UKR - Ukraine
URS - Soviet Union (1922-1992)
USA - United States of America